To Begin.

Class.

Race Conditions.

The Three Year Old Weight for Age Allowance.

Nothing but Pure Logic.

A Perfect VDW Bet.

High Win Strike Rates.

A Treble of Top Weight Penalty Carriers.

Variations on The Same Theme.

Off The Beaten Path.

A Neat Little Handicap Trick.

TO BEGIN.

Let's start by keeping it simple, firstly outlining the basic objectives within a simple formula or framework.

Firstly, we are going to isolate the best or 'Class Horse' using two proven methods.

Secondly, using a fluid measurement of performance we will be able to determine when that class horse is reaching or at the peak of its form cycle and therefore ready to do itself justice in its upcoming race.

Thirdly, once we know we have the class horse in peak physical condition we watch carefully how the clever trainers place their charges. Not only should the nominated horse be able to win by the sheer merit of its inherent ability (class) but we are also going to find further advantages through race conditions (Handicap) in which it can exploit this superiority.

I can assure the reader who is willing to use temperament and wait for the occasion when these three elements regularly align, he or she will have a selection method of some considerable force and attain winning strike rates never thought possible.

However, be warned, to discard temperament and leave out one of these factors will only lead to needless frustration. Cultivate the virtue of discipline and I assure the reader there will be plenty of occasions to reap the rewards.

CLASS.

Of course, we are all aware that in almost any sport dropping down into a lower division or league represents a drop in class and the levels of ability as a general rule are quite marked depending on the depth of class lowered or raised.

This is no different in horse racing and even a useful handicapper would usually come undone if raised into listed or group level. Never the less, this simple strategy is not to be ignored when used in conjunction with other factors of which we are about to discuss, such as, confirming the class or ability of an individual racehorse.

There is nothing quite like class on which to form a solid base or foundation for success regarding horseracing. One of the best and most underestimated methods in measuring class is what is controversially referred to in Britain as the VDW class rating, taken from the initials of a man named Van Der Whiel. This method is easy to construct for yourselves, simply by dividing the win prize money it has acquired (remember win only, not place money.) Then simply divide that figure by the total number of races it has manged to win.

In this world nothing talks quite like money! in the sphere of horse racing its influence is perhaps even greater. Let us be smart and take heed of its voice, then utilize its power to our own advantage. Please take time to mull over the three examples below. They simply illustrate how the class rating is constructed before any other factors come into play. Note, how in all three cases the value of the horses rating is higher than the value of the race it is competing in that day, giving you a reliable numerical pointer to the fact, it is now running in a lower standard of race than it has already achieved success in by winning. At least financially.

Air Pilot. Race. Goodwood, 25. September 2019. Won 6/1

Win prize money to date. £288,164. Career wins to date. 9

Divide Win Prize Money 288164 by Career Wins 9 = 32,000 or 320 (move decimal point one place to the right to get the class rating.)

Race Value to the winner on 25th September. £25,519 move decimal point one place to the right to get a rating of 255.

Air Pilots class rating 320 is much higher than the 255 race class he is competing in that day. Indicating that Air Pilot is dropping in class.

Benbatl. Race. Ascot, 27. September 2019. Won 4/1

Win prize money to date. £3,381,230. Career Wins to date. 8

Divide Win Prize Money. 3381230 by Career Wins. 8 = 4226

Benbatl class rating 4226. Race class that day. 570.

Cape Byron. Race. Ascot 5 October 2019. Won 2/1

Win Prize Money to date. £228,22 9. Career Wins to date 5

Divide Win Prize Money 228229 by 5 wins =45,645 or 456

by moving the decimal point one place to the right.

Cape Byron's Class Rating 456. Race rating that day 396 taken from £39,697 prize value to the winner.

Three straight forward bare examples, without adding any other components so as not to complicate matters. All good quality non-handicaps to keep it simple for the time being, we will get into handicaps, form cycles and much more, later.

RACE CONDITONS.

For simplicity, let us begin with another good quality non handicap race. After discerning that Min is the class horse of the race also noting that he is now dropping down in class we shall see how his trainer manages to get him a useful 'pull' at the weights.

Min. Race. Punchestown. 6 December 2020. Won 2/1.

Win Prize Money to date. £667,002. Career Wins to date 12.

667002 divided by 12 =55,5835 or a Class Rating of 555.

Race value to the winner that day £47,200 or a Rating of 472.

Mins Class Rating 555. Race Rating that day. 472.

Without doubt Min is the class horse of the race and also dropping in class from his last race. (As are all the other examples.) On the face of it, his race looks pretty straight forward. With track, going and distance in his favour.

Min has clearly shown the result is pretty favourable when he arrives from a break with form readings of 1211112 up to that point when trained by W. Mullins and an expected win is a reasonable conclusion. This also highlights another useful factor for consistent success when punting, consistent horses!

The race in which he is competing is a Grade 1 non-handicap and all the horses are to carry the same weight, in this case 11st 12lb. which at face value; is what it should be, fair. Looking closer still and we actually find the 'class horse' Min actually has a 'pull' or advantage at the official weights.

Mins official handicap rating is 169. His nearest rival on official rating is Chris's Dream at 164. Giving Min a 5lb pull on this rival despite Chris's Dream only having a class rating of 235 against Mins 555 and a race rating that day of 472 meaning Chris's Dream is going up in class amongst other disadvantages.

Allaho comes next in terms of class with a rating of 492. His official handicap rating is 160 and so despite a 63 points difference in class rating. Min still has a 9lb pull on him at the weights.

The second placed horse Tornado Flyer is also trained by Mullins. His class rating is 184 so considerably inferior when compared to Mins and with an official handicap figure of 153 means he has to concede to Min a 16lb pull in the weights.

Tornado Flyer did really well in this race and his form showed significant improvement expressed in the rise of his Top speed and Racing Post handicap ratings. This is exactly the sort of form you should be looking out for in the search for future winners. Surely, he should have been dropped in class for his next outing to collect? But I digress.

The rest of the runners really need no further comment, except that they have the same disadvantage regarding class and handicap.

The VDW class rating is a good one. When combined with advantageous race conditions, it is an excellent one! Highlighting potential profitable wagers.

Min is clearly the VDW class horse, and the race conditions are very much in his favour. His strike rate when racing after a break is impressive and it is plain for everyone to see when all these elements align the selection method is a force to be reckoned with.

Now that you have some understanding of this important relationship between class and race conditions this will give you some useful insight into what some trainers are trying to do.

In fact, at least in part, you will be forced to think like a trainer and terms such as 'penalty carrier' 'conditions race' 'weight for age' or 'sex allowance' will now cause your heart to flutter, presuming of course you have already singled out the class horse. From now on, you will be interested in like never before the details of the race conditions and pay close attention to the small print.

The chapter you just read, should now also unfold for you a new revelation,

Trainers Have the Ability to Handicap Their Own Horses! using the conditions of a race as a tool.

The Three Year Old Weight for Age Allowance.

If it were possible to isolate the best or 'class' horse of a race, just as it was peaking in its form cycle, on top of which, it has demonstrably improved to be ahead of the official handicapper. Add to this, it is now dropping into a class of race that it is easily capable of winning. And yet, as if all of these advantages are not enough, it is given yet a further weight concession sometimes up to a stone in its favour. Would that for you, look like the basis for a good bet? Maybe that bet would look like the example I am about to illustrate?

MON CHOIX made his seasonal debut on 20th June 20. but for our purposes draws no attention to himself until four races later, appearing at Windsor on 3rd August 20. Showing considerable improvement in form indicated by his Topspeed and RPR figures, not only by winning but in a race of higher class than he had ran in previously.

Other important factors to note, he was rated 72 by the official handicapper the joint second lowest rating in a 0-80 handicap. The other rated 72 was Wightman who came third carrying a 7lb claimer. The second placed horse named

Alibaba rated 78 and also carrying a claim jockey with a 3lb allowance. A further hint that Mon Choix is probably well handicapped.

Those who think that the race form is diminished by the placing of two claim jockeys, need only to look at the standard time of the race. This was only 0.22s below the standard time. The form is excellent. As are Mon Choix's form notes: 'went well clear final furlong, eased towards finish.' Winning by 7 ½ lengths. A check on Alibaba's form shows he was also coming into this race peaking in form, after winning over this CD previously and at a good standard time, only 0.12s under.

Clearly Mon Choix is well handicapped. So well handicapped in fact, his trainer will be searching in earnest to place him in a suitable race before the official handicapper gives him a hefty rise in the weights. Unless of course he had already been planning ahead.

It is also worth noting the Racing Post handicapper (RPR) awarded Mon Choix an unadjusted rating of 92 for this performance from its previous best of 74. An 18lb rise in improvement. Keeping in mind Mon Choix will only be carrying mandatory 6lb penalty, there is already a 12lb discrepancy according to him!

Mon Choix arrives at Sandown four days later. Over the same distance and most importantly on the same going. Note he is also lowered in class from a Class 4, 0-80 into a Class 5, 0-75 handicap. (a 7lb lower grade.) but the figures don't tally you may point out? Your right of course, but take a closer look.

Mon Choix is now a 78 rated horse in a 75 rated race. A further advantage! Raising his competitors' weights. Only the eventual second placed horse Delicate Kiss is less disadvantaged than the rest through being a filly and receiving her own 2lb allowance.

With his 6lb penalty already negated by dropping in grade things are looking good for Mon Choix, but he is bestowed with yet more good fortune. Note that he is a 3 year old and therefore gets a 7lb weight for age allowance for this race. An unpenalized penalty carrier if you like. No wonder he wins easily as the 10/11 favourite by 4 ½ lengths with his official handicap mark being raised by nearly a stone thereafter.

Was the above process to laborious for you? what you were really after was to just open the Racing Post, give it a quick scan and have the best bets shine out like a beacon. Am I right? Ok, I can do that. In several ways actually, but for now, just to keep things simple, let us just stick with three year olds. Only to add, we will only be interested in them if they are competing in either the second or third race of that season.

Ok, to recap, for speed and ease we are only interested in three year olds that have raced not more than twice in the current season. This is so they are fresh and ready to do justice unto themselves, under the right circumstances of course, as they have obviously wintered well and their current form has shown that they are ahead of their current official handicap rating or mark. They should win by these merits alone but we are looking for further advantages to consolidate our chances of winning. So let us take a look at how the smart trainers place these horses.

ALABAMA BOY, makes his seasonal debut at Haydock on the 24th April 21. In a Class 5, 0-75. Winning easily and receiving a hefty 10lb rise in the weights. Registering a substantial improvement from the previous season for his Topspeed figure now at 75 and his RPR at 84. Alabama Boy has clearly wintered well and trained on.

In his second race of the season at Newmarket in a Class 4, 0-80. He wins nicely again. Improving his Topspeed figure to 84 and RPR rising to 86. Note the second placed horse Freak Out officially rated 80 has a 5lb claimer, staying on well and finishing within half a length. Indicating Alabama Boy maybe well handicapped.

In the race we are going to back Alabama Boy on the 24th of June 20, he is again at Newmarket, racing over the same distance. This is a Class 4, 0-85 and at first glance Alabama Boy appears to be raised in class by 5lb plus the 3lb he has been raised by the official handicapper. However, the improving Alabama Boy in this race has a 10lb weight for age allowance and therefore all weight penalties against him thus far, have been more than negated, or to put it another way Alabama Boy runs in this race completely unpenalized. Remember, we have already considered he was well handicapped after beating a higher rated horse with a 5lb claim earlier.

And so, it comes as no surprise, that for the third time out of four races on turf, Alabama Boy wins his race as the 11/10 favourite.

It should be obvious to the reader by now, for convenience we are quickly routing out the selections, the foundation of this type of bet is actually far more complicated than it first appears. The selection methods illustrated, although effective, in reality only represent the mere framework.

Without further embellishment I would ask you to note and give some thought, to how as a two year old Alabama Boy made his debut late in the season and racing (not necessarily competing.) no more than three times. Appearing in October over 1 mile and on a grade one course in this case Newbury.

Interestingly his sire Awtaad raced only twice as a two year old debuting on a grade one course and again late in the season, over nothing less than 7 furlongs. Incidentally for only slightly different reasons than illustrated here, I backed him on his second race as a three year old. If you care to look. The same initial selection process is used.

Breeding in horseracing attracts vast amounts of money. The potential or if you prefer, scope for a horse having the ability to 'train on' obviously is a valuable trait. The shrewd punter through observation and study can profit from this. For instance, the time of year coupled with the factors just mentioned is a particularly interesting combination.

The selection procedures illustrated are viable, based on breeding, logic, class, and weight along with measurable improvement in performance. The very essence of racing.

Some of you I know, will not want to be held by restraints such as going through the form of a two year old, in order to back a three year old, let alone restricting them to 7 furlongs and over. Also, you may even quite fancy a bet on the more fraught races of the sprinters. The odds of 11/10 might not make the heart flutter either, although I assure you, bigger fish do swim along.

And so, with the above in mind and still using the same method of only looking at three year olds who are about to enter either their second or third race of the season, let us take a look at;

SPANISH ANGEL, made his seasonal debut at Goodwood on the 14th of June 2020 in a Class 3. 0-90 handicap. He is the lowest officially rated at 81. Keeping on nicely for third place within a length of the winner and indicating marked improvement through his Topspeed figure of 81, compared to the previous seasons best of 44. Also note the standard race time is good.

Within 10 days Spanish Angel is running at Windsor, a lower grade track and dropped into a Class 4, 0-85 handicap, we are going to back him. Note his official mark remained at 81. Spanish Angel as expected wins his race at odds of 3/1. But as so often happens in sprint finishes; it is not without incident. The second placed horse nearly upsetting the applecart, so let's take a closer look at this horse.

GLAMOROUS ANNA, makes her debut for the season at Windsor. In fact, in the same race as Spanish Angel makes his. Finishing last of six, when finding herself squeezed for room. Moving onto her next race, the one where she comes second to Spanish Angel, nearly colliding with the rail near the finish probably denying herself a win. However, in spite of this she does record substantial improvements in her handicap ratings, with a Topspeed figure of 74 and RPR of 88. The RPR rating of 88 is Interesting, as even after a rise from the official handicapper of 3lb he still puts her at only 85.

Glamorous Anna turns out next on the 20th July 20. Over the same course and distance also on the same going, although this time raised to a Class 3, 0-90. The highest rated horse in the field is Dachas at 87. But Glamorous Anna is the only three year old in the field and therefore gets a healthy 5lb pull in the weights due to her weight for age allowance. Glamorous Anna wins at odds of 13/2 even though it was only by a nose.

Incidentally, although the subject will be for another day, I would like to point out that Glamorous Anna in this scenario (up in class and in a sprint race,) is an outstanding candidate for a place bet. Four other horses ran with shorter odds than her. 15/8 was available on Betfair for a place. Outstanding value when you consider there were only seven runners.

Obviously sprint races bring about tighter finishes. Finding a horse with the stamina and courage to complete a mile, let alone 7 furlongs over a galloping racecourse is a whole different ball game. Hence the paragraph above with regards to the better horses coming out later in the season, nurtured along sparingly, their breeding eventually coming into play.

The reflection in greater prize money awarded to those horses that possess such attributes substantiates the point. The winner of the Derby is usually found amongst this group of horses.

Lastly, restricting yourself to a single method of selection, based in logic, such as the one we have used, will increase your chances of success considerably. Another advantage to planning and building your bets along logical lines, is that you will acquire a sense of know-how or a feel for the game. This acquisition of instinctive feel will help you bridge the gaps when the information you need is not always at hand. Once again, I will illustrate by example, albeit in a roundabout way.

CABALETTA raced only once as a two year old, winning on heavy going at Yarmouth. A flat galloping track with use of either a straight or bended mile, on the 22nd of October 2019.

Her second and debut race for the season was at Newbury on the 13th of June 2020. In a listed race for fillies over 1 mile 2 furlongs. Coming second but eventually being awarded the race as the winner was found to have a banned substance in its system. Caballeta indicating to us through her speed and handicap figures in this higher-class race, she has trained on.

Now bear with me here. Manuela De Vega as a four year old on the 7th of June 2020 debuts for the season at Haydock. Winning comfortably and indicating in the usual way how she had trained on. Her RPR of 112 being her best up to that date. On the 5th of July at the same course and slightly longer distance she was backed on the count of her being so ridiculously well handicapped. Although this was no secret as her odds of 1/2 indicated.

In that race Cabaletta came fourth some 12 lengths or so back. Even with her big weight allowance she was simply outclassed. This was also her first outing over 1 mile 4 furlongs.

The point here being, she shows no improvement in her handicap figures, running in a race at that moment in time, she had no chance of winning. But in her next race she is back at Newbury on good going and also lowered considerably in class. The conditions start to swing back in her favour and so it comes as no great leap of faith to consider she is probably still improving nicely. This time she can take advantage of her generous weight allowance. Winning in a fast time and outpacing Makawee, a five year old, who finished in front of her previously. Cabaletta's winning odds of 12/1 clearly very useful.

So, there you have it, a couple of basic guide lines can be formulated into an astounding wager.

Nothing but Pure Logic.

Ok, let us at this point review the formula and what it is exactly we are trying to achieve. Firstly, and of the uppermost importance we must isolate the 'class' or 'class horses' of any given race.

The obvious start for this is to look at horses dropping in class. This can be indicated generally when a horse is competing for lower prize money than was offered previously. Although a check should always be made that a classier horse is not lurking amongst the runners that day, either by the VDW class method as explained earlier or by a fluid measure of ability on which subject, we are about to dig a little deeper during the course of the following pages.

Any horse running with merit or showing improved form in a higher class than it has performed in previously, obviously warrants a closer look. The improvement in handicap and time figures as long as they are evaluated properly can be very illuminating. The course it has run on to achieve those figures and the number of races it has had that season for instance, may now give you more pause for thought, as you will discover.

By adapting the data from the racing papers or media from the country in which you live from the British examples I am about to reveal, will I assure, give you a steady flow of consistent winners.

Once we have satisfied ourselves, we have found a suitable candidate, we will now have to see how the trainer places it. Not only should his or her charge now be running in an inferior class but through observation they should have found an opportunity for their horse giving them a significant 'pull' in the weights or if you like, a distinct advantage on handicap.

Logic clearly tells us to be on the 'class horse' while peaking in form, before dropping class, is a sensible strategy to follow. Adding through observation of the racing rules to gain a distinct advantage at the weights then gives us a betting method of some considerable force!

Peruse the following unedited pages for further ideas and adapt for yourselves a winning plan. Please forgive any repeated articles

A Perfect VDW Bet.

In the more sedate times of the late 1970's and 1980's inspired by the now famous, Che Van Der Wheil I would dutifully collect the previous weeks race results from the now defunct Raceform Handicap Book and clip them into a folder.

Other than the obvious the main reason for doing this, as did so many others at the time, was to observe the late Ken Hussey's fantastic 'Split Second' time figures. Add to this a method of selection given to us by VDW, we could then compile a reliable list of two and three year old racehorses, with the former having the potential to enter the classics.

Read carefully the following lines: I have always favoured judging horseflesh on what it has achieves in public. This can go hand in hand with logical deductions. Keeping a horse in training is not cheap and you will note a fair number of two year olds are lightly raced in their first season. If they are kept in training it is for a good reason and the astute punter can profit by observing a few points over the first five or six weeks of the flat.

Watch closely during these first few weeks any horse that ran not more than three times as a two year old, irrespective of whether it made the frame or not, indeed it says a lot, if it was unplaced. If it gains a place 2nd or 3rd with a speed figure of 75 plus, place it in your notebook as one to follow. This process will provide with just a few bets, which if you so choose can make your profit for the flat.

There is gold in those lines and it took me an embarrassingly long time to work out why the 2nd or 3rd placed horses went into the notebook but not the winner? If you, are also not sure or cannot work it out for the moment, it will become apparent as we get deeper into this book. By the way, I would now advise if a horse wins after fulfilling the required tests, definitely add it to your list. Yes, there was a reason why he seemed to indicate only selecting the placed horses but as you will find we are going to go beyond that reason.

Later, VDW would go onto expound this method solely for the two year olds. To qualify they would need to register a 'Split Second' figure of 70 or above. This would need to be recorded on the stiff seven furlongs or better still, over the mile of one of the following grade one courses: Ascot, Doncaster, Goodwood, Newmarket, Newbury, Sandown and York. I would also now include the Curragh.

This elite list of two year olds would only amount to a few, about a half dozen or so, on which the name of the Derby winner for the following year would usually turn up. (Useful for ante-post betting.) Today you could use the Racing Post Topspeed figure of let us say not less than 90. Use the non-adjusted figures taken from the results page.

Obviously, in the United States or any other country for that matter, you will just choose and adapt the time, form and handicap figures available to you there.

Remember though, to still keep in mind those horses who have not raced more than three times late in their debut season, regardless of their speed figure or track they raced upon, as long as it was over seven furlongs or more.

As for the three year olds, their list was added to as the season progressed with further horses coming along but they were now required to register a figure of 80. Today I would suggest a Topspeed figure of 100 and above.

I can testify as have so many others, this was a very good method for consistently selecting winners just on the bare bones of its merits. Realising much later and as he pointed out himself this was only a mere framework for finding winners. Can the same be done today? The answer is yes and I will illustrate through using recent examples, but first I think it only reasonable to write a few words on temperament as this was an integral part of VDW's betting philosophy and comes into play when formulating our bet in the example.

Today we live in a time where large amounts of information are readily available and finding similar bets as described above is possible without the use of making lists. Although I would certainly not discourage this practise giving you the benefit of more time to analyse your selections. Another positive angle to making lists of horses with potential or maybe to state it more accurately, to follow a well thought out selection plan, naturally helps to instil a sense of discipline that in turn may lead to acquiring that essential quality, temperament.

VDW was adamant, until punters have acquired this indispensable asset of temperament, real success in betting would always elude them. A point it would be advisable to think upon long and hard. Many times, you will come across a horse that lacks 'all' the required credentials and you will have to leave it for another day. The compulsion to gamble is a strong one and so the ability to acquire and cultivate temperament is a requisite to a real winner. In the case of the example, I am about to give there is the potential for another horse to throw a spanner in the works. It would be most unwise to ignore it and temperament will have to come into play.

Nevertheless, if you have taken the time to gain a reasonable understanding of what you are about to undertake and just as important have acquired a feel for the game, it is possible to formulate an excellent bet on the day of the race by using only your computer. Although some may reasonably point out by not attending the actual meeting this could hold some disadvantages.

Putting that to one side, let us take a look at two horses whose paths will cross in our example. On the day we choose to back them for a win, both will be at the very peak of their form and that form will be of considerable merit. One will be described in the results summary as 'won going away' the other 'eased near finish, impressive.' Despite them both in my opinion being virtual racing certainties, they will each win at the very realistic and reasonable official odds of 9/4. After my explanation I also hope you will consider them as certainties at least as far as that word applies in racing terms.

As a two year old Adayar, (a son of Frankel.) runs only twice both times at Nottingham and both times on soft going. (Easy on the joints.) Firstly, on the 14th of October 2020, interestingly as the 11/5 favourite, over 1 mile ½ furlong. Finishing sixth after starting slowly. Second time out was over the same distance on the 28th of October. This time Adayar wins at the odds of 3/1 by nine lengths, taking the lead from 3 furlongs out. The Topspeed figure achieved was an excellent 90 on this galloping track and the RPR a respectable 97 and so he makes it onto our list.

For the 2021 season as a three year old, note how Adayar's form notes read as he is gradually increased in distance. consistently mentioning his willingness to run on strongly from over two furlongs out. Just as he did in his third race, when we get really interested in him, winning no less a race than the English Derby! (The 11/8 favourite Bolshoi Ballet at the time of writing still not within five lengths of winning a twelve furlong race.)

Adayars Topspeed figure soars to 116 and his RPR to 124. Marking our card. Now, we will have to figure out, after showing his class to win The Derby, will he have the class to win The King George VI, where he will be contesting older horses. taking no more than a cursory glance at the field and a possible fly in the ointment glaringly stands out in the shape of the classy Mishriff. The multi million prizes for the Arabian prizes he won make the class element hard to assess as they are so astronomically out of kilter when compared to the paltry half a million Adayar received for winning the English Derby as a comparison.

Another aspect of Mishriff's form to be aware of is, this will be his second race after a 98 day break, readers of my VDW Missing Link book, will already know how I favour this scenario, under the right circumstances of course.

I will eventually get to why Adayar is an outstanding bet for this race, but so is Mishriff, at least for a place! Two places, in fact! Never finishing out of the first two on good or better going. His three worst positions so far, are in races taking place in October. His next worst position 3rd was in July but that was on good to soft. Winning 7 and coming 2nd twice in his remaining 9 races outside of those unfavourable factors. And yet, still able to manage a win on heavy going. Mishriff is an outstanding place bet at odds of up to 6/4 with his 100% success rate under these conditions.

Now, we shall return to Adayar, racing at Ascot for the King George VI, at the pinnacle of his form after previously registering a Topspeed figure not yet achieved by Mishriff.

We know the how and why he deserves to be in this race, but let us look a little deeper into the form of his Derby win for confirmation. Firstly, we see he had to overcome an awkward start, which gives us ground for expecting further improvement, should any be needed? Taking the lead over 2 furlongs out, being ridden clear, over 1 furlong out, staying on strongly. All good stuff. The Racing Post standard time for this race is slow by 0.85s so not too bad either.

Turning our attention now to the race at Ascot and clearly Adayar, on that day and at that moment is the horse most likely to win. But is all this enough for us to wager on him?

Of course, it isn't! No, we need a further advantage, just to make sure everything is in his/our favour! and for this we scrutinise the race conditions. Since we consider Mishriff the principal threat, we note his official handicap mark is 122 making him 1lb superior to Adayar, and yet in this race Adayar is carrying a very healthy 11lb less than Mishriff.

This is because he is a three year old and gets a weight for age allowance. This is a huge drag on Mishriff, especially for the time of year, so much so, that Adayar wins 'going away.' His job for us is done, Adayar is now put away for betting purposes.

Never the less, Mishriff has run extremely well, and as expected maintained his 100% record finishing in the first two places. (No guessing for us.) and so we get paid. Twice!

Mishriff has run so well in fact, he has recorded his best ever Topspeed figure, a lofty 116. He has now marked our card for us, in the same way Adayar did previously. Mishriff is now at the pinnacle of his form and therefore attracts our full attention.

Peering deeper into his King George form, we are already aware of his weight disadvantage with the winner, but note also, the third placed horse Love who has a filly's allowance giving her a 3lb pull on him. But to be fair, why Love was the

13/8 favourite up against the big boys and over that distance, I'm not quite sure?

Steadied at the start and held up in last place, until <u>making headway on the outer,</u> certainly shows Mishriff is a versatile horse and on that day covered more ground than was necessary. Especially when we find the Racing Post standard time for the race is fast by 2.56s.

The tactics used for him in this race show the trainer/connections were aware of his considerable weight disadvantage and clearly tried to conserve his energy. This is excellent form.

Mishriff is entered for the Group 1 Juddmonte International Stakes. Straight away we can discard the second favourite Love as a contender for the same reasons mentioned earlier, even though she has 3 ½ furlongs less to run, but that also applies to Mishriff.

The third favourite Alcohol Free, has no chance on distance alone. The horse who eventually came second in this race Alenquer is a three year old as are some of the other runners but in every case the weights are definitely in Mishriff's favour. Alenquer rated a 14lb inferior horse to Mishriff and yet through race conditions only receives half of that weight allowance, effectively giving the already superior Mishriff a 7lb pull in the weights. In the race itself, Mishriff leaves his competitors trailing in his wake as the 9/4 favourite. For the VDW followers both examples are classic cases of using the 'missing link' element, that and utilising the mostly reliable form of CLASS HORSES.

I think you will agree, all so far is thought provoking stuff and for those that have read and understood how the bets were put together or if you prefer, formulated, only the horses I highlighted could possibly have been considered as candidates for the winners' enclosure.

Mishriff at first presented us with a problem and he could easily have jeopardised our bet on Adayar. However, through the use of Temperament and careful consideration of the statistics/odds, we turn this problem instead to our advantage. Making the overall wager on this race some might refer to as a 'bet to nothing.'

Adayar was clearly the horse holding the key advantages in that race. However, to those who are serious about making a profit from the game, Mishriff should have posed a very interesting question. Is betting on a horse for a place a viable proposition? Or you may ask the question in a different way. What if it were Mishriff carrying all those advantages of the winner, should he still be backed for a place? The answer is an emphatic yes! In fact, if you believe he is going to win, then for a place, you should be putting twice as much money on him!

By the way, did you figure out why VDW only required the two year olds, to make the frame 2nd or 3rd but not necessarily to win, when making the list? I believe it was so they did not have to carry a penalty into the following season or more cynically, perhaps their trainers did not want the official handicapper to get too excited over the ability of their charge.

Finally, Adayar proved the criteria set, in order to get onto our list of select two year olds, has significant merit! His official rating of 108 and even dropping to 107 for the Derby in hindsight now looks very lenient. A full stone or 14lbs being added to his ratings thereafter. However, for having read this book, you have now become astute punters! Noting in the King George, where we backed him, all his weight raised was in fact negated through race conditions. Adayar was clearly ahead of official ratings at that particular time of his life. But the really exciting point to all this is, now you know why!

High Win Strike Rates.

Recently I wrote a book with the obscure title, VDW 'Missing Link' Solved. This title relates to a man named Che Van der Wheil, who in the late 1970's illustrated for the readers of the now defunct Raceform Handicap Book, a method of singling out the Class/Form horse of a race, and therefore the one most likely to win.

Firstly, taking the first six runners of the betting forecast, he would utilise their form figures to form a numerical picture, highlighting the three most consistent runners.

He would then go on to isolate the 'Class horse' from the six runners by dividing their Win prize monies against their career wins achieved. If the horse with highest class rating, aligned with one of the form horses, it could be then considered as a possible bet. VDW then went on to say, by using restraint and temperament, it was possible to have wining strike rates of 70% or even better, after taking other things into consideration.

This proven formula for isolating the 'probables' was well accepted, and I think it fair to say, still is! Some of the readers were doing very well, and could not praise VDW enough. However, for the majority misunderstandings were soon to come. What were these other things, to be taken into consideration? This generated hundreds of letters to the reader's page. Yes, they now knew how to isolate the Class/Form horse, but how could they tell, when it was in a position to take advantage of its circumstance? Or in racing terms, when could it be considered as a racing certainty?

In the book mentioned I explained exactly how this was done. However, in these few pages I would like to illustrate for you by example, another way of isolating the 'Class horse.' Then we will look to see, if it has been placed to win. That is to ask, are the conditions of the race overwhelmingly in its favour? As you will see with, Missunited on the two occasions we back her, she had already attained a success rate of 100%

MISSUNITED, after a 164 day break is turned out at Limerick, on the 10th April 2014 coming third of three, as the 4/9 favourite. Next time out is at Ascot, she is up in class running in a group 3, with a prize to the winner of £34k. Coming fourth of ten, and showing improvement in her handicap ratings with a Topspeed figure of 65 and Postmark figure of 97.

Her following race is at Leopardstown, where she is dropped in class to a listed race worth £26k to the winner. Where she wins at the odds of 9/2. Registering improvement in her figures, once again. Topspeed 68 Postmark 106. The question here is, should she be backed in this race? The answer is yes! For a place! (Bear with me.)

For her next race, Missunited is raised considerably in class and distance. This is at Ascot in a Group 1, worth £212k to the winner, running over two miles, four furlongs.

Missunited finished second by half a length. (Stewards Inquiry.) However, there is now a marked improvement in her handicap figures Topspeed 82 Postmark 115. Obviously, Miss United is coming to the boil. A closer look at the form reveals she 'found extra 3 furlongs out.' Not 1 or 2, but 3 furlongs out! This is extremely relevant, for obvious reasons. Especially if we take a deeper dive into the form. The Racing Post standard race time was fast by 0.41s

You can look up for yourselves regarding the intricacies. But to quickly summarise, the RP standard time is an average of the 10 best times over the last five seasons for a mature horse rated (BHA) at 100, carrying 9 stones on good ground. This solidly substantiates for us the validity and merits of Missuniteds form. Any horse finding 'extra' 3 furlongs out in a race of this quality and at the time set, is beyond doubt a 'Class' horse!

We can see that Missunited has now, all the attributes of a winner, but still needs to be placed in the company she is capable of exploiting.

Missunited, on the 31st July 2014 arrives at Goodwood. Dropping two grades in class into a Group 3 race worth £34k to the winner, over the reduced distance of 1 mile 6 furlongs, after consideration of the facts presented so far, she is starting to look like a worthy bet. However, more confirmation is still needed and for the readers of my first book, you will further see why VDW insisted upon backing the better class racehorses, enabling him to achieve a consistently high strike rate of winners.

To date Missunited had raced over 1 mile 6 furlongs six times, on all types of going, either winning or coming second. (A strike rate of 100% for the first two places.) VDW himself confirmed he would often back two or more horses to ensure a profit. We no longer have that headache as Betfair allows us to back horses for a place. Often at excellent value odds.

Missunited looked all over the eventual winner, but in the class element, there is a threat in Talent. A substantial place bet (for me) was placed, at odds of 4/6 down to 1/2 and a smaller amount for a win, remember her first two placings at this distance so far stands at 100%. And we now have her primed, Missunited won at the official odds of 3/1fav.

When verifying for yourselves these selections on the Racing Post website, you will find that the form for this race is not without drama. Putting that to one side, the race happens to throw up another candidate for a possible bet in the future.

Going off track here, so I will only mention briefly why I think the second placed horse, Arabian Comet was a very good 'place bet' for her next race. As a three year old, even with her age allowance, racing over such a long distance, against older horses this was an outstanding performance. Her form reading certainly shows she is a trier. Against lesser horses, over a shorter distance next time out, could arguably be deemed as unlucky not to win, agonisingly losing by only a nose at a price of 9/2 and Evens for a place. Take a look for yourselves and see what you think?

A Treble of Top Weight Penalty Carriers.

Raising the weight/class of their rivals while dropping in class themselves.

For those amongst you who would prefer to specialize. (A strategy in and of itself that would improve your chances of success considerably.) Then penalty carriers are a group of horses well worth consideration. Even so, as always in racing other factors will have a bearing and there are many to consider.

Some trainers are better than others at placing their charges to win for instance. The time of year has a huge influence that goes unnoticed by the majority (Note, the first three examples given in this book.) But I will leave that subject for later.

Instead, concentrate on the title of this chapter by example.

True Pleasure. 8th April. 2015. Won a 0-75 Handicap race at Catterick over 7 furlongs by a 'keeping on well' three lengths, this was <u>her</u> second race from a 55 day break. Showing considerable improvement in form as indicated by her Racing Post handicap and Topspeed figures.

This improvement did not go unnoticed by the stewards and an explanation was required, which you can read for yourself in the form summary notes. Note the next three positions were taken by higher officially rated male horses, geldings in fact. Note also, two of them had 5lb claimers and one of them was the second favourite. This is relevant information when the possibility of True Pleasures next race could be that of a 6lb penalty carrier.

True Pleasures next race came on the 15th of April at Beverley over an extended mile. Dropping in class to a 0-70 Fillies Handicap.

This time around True Pleasure has only to compete against her own sex of which the highest officially rated was only 65.

Although True Pleasure carried 9st 13lb in this race she was still 'well in.' In fact, by my own calculations, she was very well handicapped!

In the previous years it is also well worth noting how well, True Pleasure performed carrying heavy weights on galloping tracks with uphill finishes and in races of class, she had no chance of winning.

Al Khan. Was making his seasonal debut and winning at Catterick on the 22nd April 2015 in a Class 3 0-90 Handicap.

His Racing Post and Topspeed figures show he has come out of the winter in excellent condition and ahead of the game. This gives me the opportunity to introduce another very useful element that can be used to add further confirmation to your evaluation of form, that is the Racing Post standard time found at bottom of the form summary in the results pages.

The standard time he set for the race was slow by 0.38s so very good, especially for a handicapper on debut and even taking into consideration it was on good to firm.

The standard time explained very loosely is: The 10 best times recorded in the past 5 seasons by a standard BHA horse rated 100 and carrying 9st on good going. This for me is a wonderful aid to the serious punter in gauging whether or not the race you are evaluating is good reliable form.

Al Khan re-appears at Ayr on the 27th of April. Winning at odds of 9/4 carrying a 6lb penalty and therefore dropped to a Class 4, 0-85 from a Class 3, 0-90 presumably to negate 5lbs from his penalty and hopefully gain an edge in class.

Note here Al Khan is rated 88 in an 80 race and consequently pulling his adversaries out of their comfort zone with regards to carrying weight.

(Truthfully, did you notice the same scenario in the True Pleasure example?) And speaking of truth, in Al Khans first race described by me, the horse second to him was Regal Dan also running for the same trainer. Although not a penalty carrier in his next race, he just failed to win and I lost that particular wager by a nose. Never the less, I mention it as you may wish to study that race to gain further insight into my methods.

However, getting back to the point and our present examples. Earlier you may recall I wrote that trainers have the ability to handicap their own horses. But we could also put it another way 'that trainers have the ability to handicap other trainers' horses.' As shown by these examples.

I will try to make my case with a more straight forward example as we try to gain some insight in seeing what the trainer of Landing Night is up to when placing his horse after a win, as a top weight penalty carrier.

Landing Night, arrives at Catterick in a Class 4, 0-80 Handicap on the 29th of May with steady improvement in form after an 83 day break. Culminating in a win and achieving a Raceform handicap figure of 79 and a Topspeed figure of 71 both the best of his career thus far, therefore indicating he is in peak form.

Landing Night is only carrying 8st 8lb and has a very useful 9lb weight for age allowance being only 3 years old, but not the only 3 year old in that race.

A note here: Landing Night did not have a clear run 2 furlongs out and showed superb courage to squeeze between two rivals 1 furlong out before soon leading, and driven out to win. This is an excellent form reading and some might say a measure of class.

Appearing again seven days later and again at Catterick, which is obviously helpful. This time however, dropping into to 10lb lower grade. A Class 5, 0-70 Handicap. Keeping in mind he is now rated 75.

 Meaning not only has he already shown he can beat higher officially rated horses entered in this race, but being the highest officially rated horse he has drawn all his rivals' weight upwards. Effectively raising them in class. However, this time around he is the only 3 year old in the race and thus receives a further helpful 7lb pull in the weights due to his weight for age allowance.

 Simply put, by ratings standard he is justifiably the best horse in the race, but gets a 7lb bonus pull by virtue of his trainers' canny observation of the race conditions. No wonder he won on the bit over 2 furlongs out.

Just because a horse is carrying top weight does not mean, it cannot be still well handicapped.

Ok, the odds of 5/6 mean he was not overlooked but the insight into the trainers thinking is of considerable interest and as with the other examples, we can put these same ideas in to use, also gaining more rewarding odds.

Variations on The Same Theme.

Just to recap here, what it is we are trying to achieve. In all examples; applying various selection methods, using nothing but simple logic we single out the class horse in the field. Aligning this at a time, when its form is 'blooming' to use a different term of expression than usual.

 To compound the advantages of our chosen class horse, we then search out for any discrepancies in the weights even though it appears to be already ahead of its own official handicap mark. Equally and just as important, after considering these advantages, it needs to be placed in a class of race, that it is more than capable of winning.

Lead a Merry Dance. Makes her seasonal debut at Bath racecourse on the 13th of May 2015 in a Class 5, 0-75 Fillies Handicap.

Showing the classic signs, she has trained on by registering considerable improvement in her Racing Post handicap figures from a best of 57 from the previous season to that of 81 on her first race of this one.

It is important to note also, that all her rivals in this race hold an official handicap mark higher than her own, and that Glastonberry the odds on favourite she beat into second place had a 7lb claiming jockey and was 'unpenalized' from its previous race win, as that was an apprentice riders race! (Remember?) Indeed, the third placed horse Edged Out also had a 7lb claiming jockey and yet, Lead a Merry Dance won this race by 3 ¾ lengths, ridden clear then being eased in the last 75 yards. An obvious candidate to become a penalty carrier.

Lead a Merry Dance is next seen 7 days later at Goodwood on the 21st of May 2015 in a 0-70 Apprentice Handicap so dropping down 5lb in class and this time she is ridden by a 5lb claimer. Don't forget she has already beaten higher officially rated horses in the previous race than there are in today's and they were using 7lb claimers. A turnaround of 17lb in weight? Hitting the front over one furlong out and soon in command, Lead a Merry Dance wins as the 6/4 favourite.

Can we get winners with higher odds using these methods? Some of you may be asking, the answer is yes and to illustrate I will switch racing codes to the jumps and give another interesting 'tweak' on how we can find a well handicapped candidate.

No No Cardinal. Had gone twenty-three races without even looking as though he could win a race but in race number twentyfour, he showed a couple of things that now; for us at least, would make us look twice.

Coming out from a long break of 204 days the interestingly named No No Cardinal shows up at Chepstow on the 1st of May 2015 at a price of 66/1 finishing an uninspiring fourth of five runners, 39 lengths behind the winner. Only managing a miserable Raceform Handicap figure of 11.

He is out again only six days later at Wincanton another galloping track on the 7th of May 2015 showing a surprising transformation, finishing a 1 ½ length second in an eventful race, with the probable winner falling at the last, and worth noting this horse Agapanthus won six days later.

But closer examination of the form shows No No Cardinal being held up and 'making headway 4 out' while carrying '6lb overweight' against higher rated horses on a galloping track but getting to the 'last' and finishing one paced on the run in.

No No Cardinal recorded his best Topspeed figure to date of 82 with a Raceform Handicap figure of 81.

Newton Abbott 27ᵗʰ May 2015. No No Cardinal is still carrying overweight only 2lb this time around and a little better off with his previous victor All But Grey the 5/1 favourite for this race. I understand that a good case can be made for All But Grey as a probable winner and at the odds it would have been easy to back the two. However, it also worth noting this was to be All But Greys eighth race since coming from a break.

Having a horse come from a galloping track to sharp one when hitting peak form is one of my favourite scenarios. With his bottom weight of only 10 stone and this time only having to contend with a short run in.

For me this was always going to be No No Cardinals Day and on the Betfair market you could have got much better odds than the 9/1 shown on official results.

Another national hunt horse winning around the same time was Minne Milan not so generous with the odds this time but another runner I considered a certainty in racing terms. Coming from an 83 day break showing a pleasing steady climb in Racing Post and Topseed figures and we will join her at the apex of her form.

Minnie Milan, Comes to Uttoxeter on the 16ᵗʰ of May 2015 winning a 0-120 Mares Handicap at odds of 5/1.

Taking the lead '3 out' and drawing away at the finish against the much higher rated Ebony Empress (whom, I suspect was 'really' meant to win this?) Never the less, not only was Ebony Empress rated a massive 25lb superior horse to Minnie Milan on official ratings but as I'm sure you've guessed by now, was ridden by a 7lb claim jockey.

The third placed horse Maypole Lass rated 10lb superior but never the less was still 5 ½ lengths adrift of the winner.

Minne Milan's Racing Post handicap figure jumped from 72 to a substantial 102 and from 91 to another 102 for his Topspeed rating. Now we know at least potentially, Minnie Milan is very well handicapped but, we still need that final ingredient from the trainer that ensures her chances of a win and gives us the green light for placing a bet.

May the 26th 2015 Huntingdon and Minnie Milan is dropped in class from a 0-120 handicap to a much lower one rated 0-105. Where she wins comfortably as the 5/2 favourite on this flatter and faster track.

Ok, so I am sure you have got the idea by now. Only to add one more comment. If your chosen horse of the day is running on a much sharper track than the previous one and also over a longer distance. See this in the main, as a good thing.

The earlier example of No No Cardinal with only an extra furlong to run on a sharper track, gave him a chance to 'amplify' his class on that particular day, making headway at the seventh, before taking the lead after four out, keeping on well to the finish. Or to put it another way, allowed him in that particular race, on that particular day 'to go harder for longer.'

Off The Beaten Path.

So far, in the previous chapters I have grouped two sets of horses. Taken from my notes, albeit separated by a gulf in this matter of class.

The first three examples were to illustrate in the most black and white terms, the long sort after answer for some, to finding the so called VDW missing link or key, as it has been described over the years.

How do I know my explanation is the right answer? Easy, in his letter to the Raceform Handicap Book dated 13th April 1985. He actually tells you, writing '… providing you READ

WHAT WAS THERE; The last in capital letters because it was all there although a vital factor, call it the missing link if you like was not deliberately pointed out. It is there for you to see and it was not covered up, but until you approach the problem in the right way the odds are it will remain obscure. Once you find it everything will be so clear that you will wonder how on earth you could miss it and you will have the same horses as myself.'

Adding little clues for us in the same letter by using the analogy of buying a train ticket 'We all want to get to the same destination but there is no obligation to board the same transport or go via the same route, what matters is that you arrive. Therefore, it is advisable to read the small print on the ticket, it will contain things which are not at first apparent.

Hmm, could this small print be the race conditions set above every race card?

He then gave three further examples of his methods and even mentions their individual advantage in the weights but purposely and interestingly does not elaborate on this factor in any shape or form what so ever, only ever writing 'pull in the weights but no mention why they would have this pull. Leaving it up to the readers to research for themselves.

This I managed to do, only with a bit of luck, finding old race results in second hand book and charity shops.

The second group of horses I used as examples do not possess anything like near the level of ability of the first and just the ambition of recording a win will be enough to tax their trainer's skill and imagination.

Which opens the door for us to exploit their ideas in order for us to gain some profit. I have several ways of going about this, but the ones I displayed for you were done to maintain some uniformity, done this way we can keep things simple. They were all backed for the same reasons over and over. For instance, the penalty carriers were not just penalty carriers but all were top weight penalty carriers and all within a seasonal time frame.

Time of the year, for the majority in racing means searching the optimum time period for when a particular horse does his winning. This of course is relevant information and should not be overlooked.

However, there can be no one on the planet who does not recognize the natural radiance effecting nature in the spring time and early summer. The horses illustrated clearly had wintered well but in their public performances they were also expressing a natural exuberance for this magical time of year, responding to it more so than their rivals. In my opinion.

Looking at the results more thoroughly and seeing how trainers sometimes respond by placing their charges up in class rather than down, presumably liking what they see on the gallops. It can certainly be an educational read, all the while keeping in mind the time of year.

The bonus of study should offer a valuable insight into the methods of that particular trainer. After all, you and they would surely welcome, the powerful force of nature assisting you, when placing a horse to win.

In fact, incorporating this force of nature would sometimes allow you to place some substantial wagers with high confidence indeed of a return, even when going up in class, some horses stand out like a sore thumb.

Southfield Vic after a 173 day break turns out at Fontwell racecourse on the 21st of April 2017 in a tight little three runner affair.

These races are usually slow making the form suspect but reading the excellent form summary showing Southfield Vic romping around the course, jumping well and winning super comfortably by 23 lengths. The standard race time was slow by 6 seconds. This is acceptable at a distance of well over three miles considering his jumping was superb and how Southfield Vic easily drew clear. Room for any amount of improvement, if needed.

Recording a Raceform handicap figure of 156 with a Topspeed figure of 130 is impressive enough, even on this low grade track and coming from a long break.

Southfield Vic turns out at Newton Abbott 19 days later. Up from a class 4 novice chase to a class 3 handicap chase. Interestingly on this day Southfield Vic was also the top rated VDW horse in this race. The other runners never stood a chance. Winning very easily as the 9/4 favourite by 24 lengths recording his best Racing Post handicap and Topspeed figures to date of 159 and 134.

Southfield Vic under those circumstances was incredibly well handicapped on that day. Only to add the Racing Post Handicapper rated his performance at Fontwell at 156 and yet his official rating at Newton Abbott was only 140 if you were to read them as a direct comparison. Which I believe is the idea.

Another point worth making is that once we have collected Southfield Vic is put away for betting purposes and the same goes for all the other horses highlighted in this book. The reason is very straightforward. They don't win often enough afterwards, simple as that!

This does not mean you can't back the second placed horse to your selection of the day because obviously we know, our horse is well in advance of its official handicap rating.

For example, referring back to my notes under the section of what I call 'in the family' (meaning horses getting close enough to my own selection.)

Noble Friend was a horse of interest to me on the 9th of March 2015. Displaying marked improvement in form while racing at Plumpton in a Class 4 handicap rated 0-115 beating a horse called Sportsreport who was officially rated 101 carrying a 3lb claimer while Noble Friend was only rated 97.

Noble Friend was back at Plumpton on April the 5th 2015 dropped to a Class 4 0-105 now rated at 104 he won at 3/1. Although as usual I got higher odds on Betfair.

Reviewing the result later I saw that the second placed horse **My Silver Cloud** was only rated 79. But more significantly was 10lb out of the handicap. Despite this he finished within a neck of my winning horse and beat the rest of the field who were rated 105 down to 102. Meaning My Silver Cloud was placed in my notebook of horses to look out for in the future.

You know what I'm about to say don't you?

My Silver Cloud posted his best Racing Post Handicap figure that day and second best of Topspeed. He had been entered in some ridiculously out of reach races in his career.

 Not in his next race however, which was at Fontwell on the 10th of April. He was entered in a lower Class 5, 0-100 Handicap. Not only that, he is now officially rated at 69 and in the handicap proper. Even though we know he has just beaten horses rated over 100 while out of the handicap rated at 79 only 5 days earlier.

My Silver Cloud started as the 6/4 favourite leading from the eighth fence out and even after veering left after two fences out, staying on well to win.

Illustrating that although previously My Silver Cloud came with in a neck of a much superior officially rated horse, and a well handicapped horse at that! He still has to tick the boxes of our winner finding check list before meriting as a worthy selection.

Churchtown Champ on the 19th of October 2016 turned out at Worcester after a 204 day break. Improving off the scale with his best ever Topspeed figure of 108 and Raceform Handicap rating of 136. Coming second to a horse officially rated 4lb superior and ridden by a 3lb claimer. The horse coming third helped to confirm the form, as he was officially rated 7lbs superior.

Next time Churchtown Champ is entered in a limited handicap race at Southwell on the 15th November 2016 in a same class race however, this race contained lower officially rated horses.

Once again, as in the previous example our horse is running on a sharp track coming from a galloping one last time. It also has an extra furlong and 3 extra fences to clear, which should help emphasise Churchtown Champs class.

Winning by 10 lengths and heavily eased as the 5/4 favourite having only to beat a horse rated 128 this time. This horse was called,

Pearl Swan although 10 lengths behind the well handicapped Churchtown Champ, was upsides three fences out before hitting it and keeping on to the line. Not bad, since he was coming from a 389 day break. Pearl Swan was lowered 1lb from his mark for this effort. (A helpful difference of opinion.)

Looking back through his career, it is obvious to see he was being entered in races where he was hopelessly out of his depth.

Ffoss Llass on the 30th of November 2016. Pearl Swan was at last, entered into a race he was capable of winning. Dropped into a Class 4 Novice Chase. He did just that at odds of 7/2 making all and even increasing the pace from the tenth.

A Neat Little Handicap Trick of My Own.

Here is a useful little trick that I devised for myself, this can be used as either a basis for selection in its own right or help you decide upon whether a horse is carrying too much weight against that day's competition.

Keeping in mind always, it is only to be used as a helpful guide while incorporating other selection methods as described earlier and not as a stand-alone winner finding method. Never the less, I am certain you will find it very interesting as well as effective.

Go Dan Go, raced at Carlisle racecourse on the 24th June 2015. Winning after being dropped in class but was still of interest after showing improvement, recording very good Racing Post handicap and Topspeed figures, his best ever in fact.

Ten days later Go Dan Go is back at Carlisle over 1 furlong less and with a revised official handicap mark 6lb higher in the same class of race as last time but for three year olds only.

This method compares against the two horses you consider dangers to your own. You can compare more but for simplicity it will be best to give an example first, and go from there.

Note, as in the penalty carrier examples Go Dan Go is rated 91 in a 0-85 race. And therefore, raising the weights of his rivals. Let us take the first three placings as they finished noting they were in fact the market leaders. Alongside is their handicap mark rating.

Go Dan Go   91

Special Venture   75

Johnny B Goode   75

Looking at the previous form of the 2nd and 3rd placed horses as indeed the 4th they were all coming into this race as serious contenders to win.

The ratings indicate a 16lb difference in the weights meaning even at 2lb a length Go Dan Go has the potential to win this by 8 lengths, possibly more? Who knows? So, what to do?

Let us take the 16lb and turn it into 15lb to make things easy, before simply dividing it by 3. Or 15 divided by 3 = 5 or 5lb.

Then call these 5lbs improvement or deterioration to make things harder for Go Dan Go we will take 5lb from his rating and instead reward the other two with the 5lb making a difference or turnaround of 10lb, like so,

Go Dan Go   86 from official rating 91 deteriorated 5lb?

Special Venture   80 from official rating 75 improved 5lb?

Johnny B Goode   80 from official rating 75 improved 5lb?

As the ratings now stand. We have implied that Go Dan Go has deteriorated by 5lb, even though we know different. Adding further hinderance to him on paper at least, we then give 5lb each as improvement to both his rivals. I make this a 10lb turnaround in the weights against Go Dan Go.

And yet, even after these 'unfair' adjustments we still see that he has a 6lb advantage on the figures.

If you considered that the fourth placed Mythmaker was a bigger threat than say Johnny B Goode simply replace him in the equation. This would now show that Mythmaker has a 1lb advantage over Go Dan Go.

However, you would have to weigh up the fact how the scales have been tipped to get Mythmaker this 1lb advantage. Also, that he has never won over seven furlongs or with the word soft in the going.

 This was the best placement on his trainers' part as he had improved very nicely up to that point. This was noted and he was backed for his next race over 6 furlongs on firm going for all the reasons you are now familiar with. Winning at 9/2.

Obviously, application of this method has its limitations, but when the situation arises and it can be brought into play, it is a very useful tool indeed. Widening and making the view clearer for the punter.

For older readers who may remember the Roushayd example given by VDW when winning the Old Newton Cup in 1988 explaining the value of speed figures as an ingredient to winner finding. I will add a further point that you may find interesting? By first laying out the weights of the first three placed horses, who were also the market leaders, followed by their official handicap mark number.

Roushayd	9st 10lb	96
Il De Chypre	8st 10lb	94
Vouchsafe	8st 11lb	83

A difference of 16lb between the lowest and highest rated horse in actual weight carried. Note: there is only 2lb difference in official ratings of the top two but Il De Chypre has a very generous weight for age allowance by virtue of being a three year old and understandably an obvious favourite for the race.

Under these race conditions Roushayd's chances of winning already look extremely difficult. However, once again forget the odds and sods by rounding up the number of weight difference to 15lb for convenience, then divide this number by 3 giving us the answer of 5 or in our case 5lb. We will then deny Roushayd his 5lb improvement and instead call it deterioration. The other two horses we will then reward, giving 5lb to each and call it improvement. A further 10lb disparity against Roushayd, so the adjusted figures now look like this, at least in weight to be carried.

Roushayd   9st 5lb

Il De Chypre 8st 13lb

Vouchsafe   9st 2lb

Roushayd still comes out on top in our adjusted, actual weight to be carried rating, despite Il De Chypres huge weight for age allowance. The final use of ratings is it not, to have something to look at? Ok, I'm being a little glib. But I am sure you would agree, it is an interesting read, especially when taking other factors into consideration.

I am just putting the idea out there, as it has certainly helped me when dealing with topweights and their chances. Maybe some of you can push the ball further and improve on this idea?

Ok, I hope you have enjoyed my little book. The examples taken from my notes are there to show, that just by using simple logic you can muster up some very useful methods to aid winner finding.

For example, just by using simple observation and logic you can attain a very high strike rate of winners within certain areas of horse racing. But you have to wait for these occasions to arise or as VDW put it, exercise temperament.

Speaking of VDW the 'missing link 'saga I know has gone on for many years. Some saying they have found the link and have even found ways to extort money by it, without ever revealing what it is they have supposed to have discovered.

So, for the price of this little book revealing such a treasure I am sure you will agree, it represents pretty good value.

Printed in Great Britain
by Amazon

40609102R00033